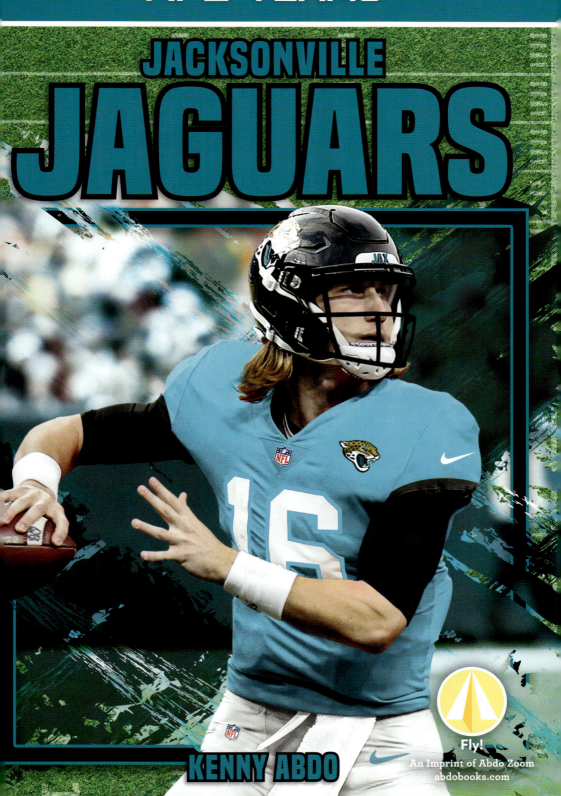

abdobooks.com

Published by Abdo Zoom, a division of ABDO, P.O. Box 398166, Minneapolis, Minnesota 55439. Copyright © 2022 by Abdo Consulting Group, Inc. International copyrights reserved in all countries. No part of this book may be reproduced in any form without written permission from the publisher. Fly!™ is a trademark and logo of Abdo Zoom.

Printed in the United States of America, North Mankato, Minnesota.
052021
092021

Photo Credits: Alamy, Getty Images, Icon Sportswire, iStock, newscom, Shutterstock PREMIER
Production Contributors: Kenny Abdo, Jennie Forsberg, Grace Hansen
Design Contributors: Candice Keimig, Neil Klinepier

Library of Congress Control Number: 2020919503

Publisher's Cataloging-in-Publication Data

Names: Abdo, Kenny, author.
Title: Jacksonville Jaguars / by Kenny Abdo
Description: Minneapolis, Minnesota : Abdo Zoom, 2022 | Series: NFL teams | Includes online resources and index.
Identifiers: ISBN 9781098224653 (lib. bdg.) | ISBN 9781098225599 (ebook) | ISBN 9781098226060 (Read-to-Me ebook)
Subjects: LCSH: Jacksonville Jaguars (Football team)--Juvenile literature. | National Football League--Juvenile literature. | Football teams--Juvenile literature. | American football--Juvenile literature. | Professional sports--Juvenile literature.
Classification: DDC 796.33264--dc23

TABLE OF CONTENTS

Jacksonville Jaguars 4

Kick Off. 8

Team Recaps 14

Hall of Fame 24

Glossary 30

Online Resources 31

Index 32

JACKSONVILLE JAGUARS

Stalking the field dressed in gold, black, and teal, the Jacksonville Jaguars have a fierce competitiveness for victories!

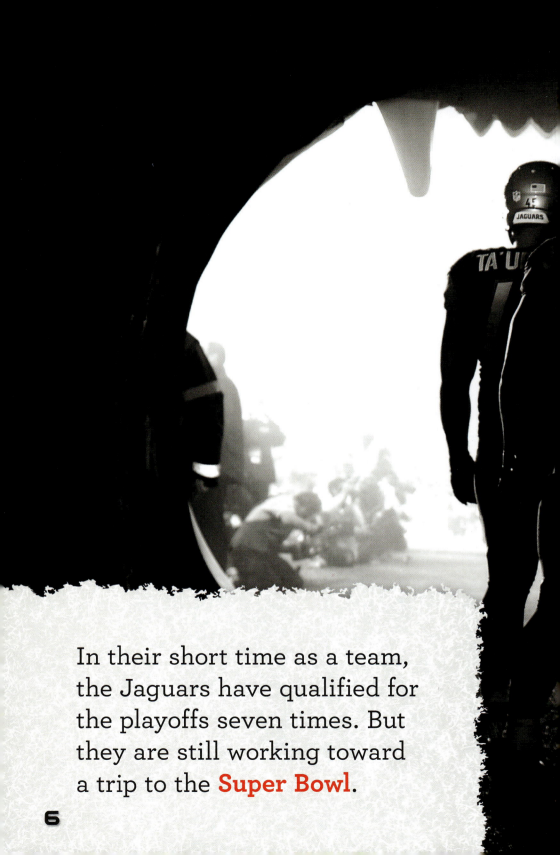

In their short time as a team, the Jaguars have qualified for the playoffs seven times. But they are still working toward a trip to the **Super Bowl**.

KICK OFF

In 1989, the Touchdown Jacksonville! group wanted to bring an NFL team to the Florida city. Jacksonville was one of five cities in the running by 1992.

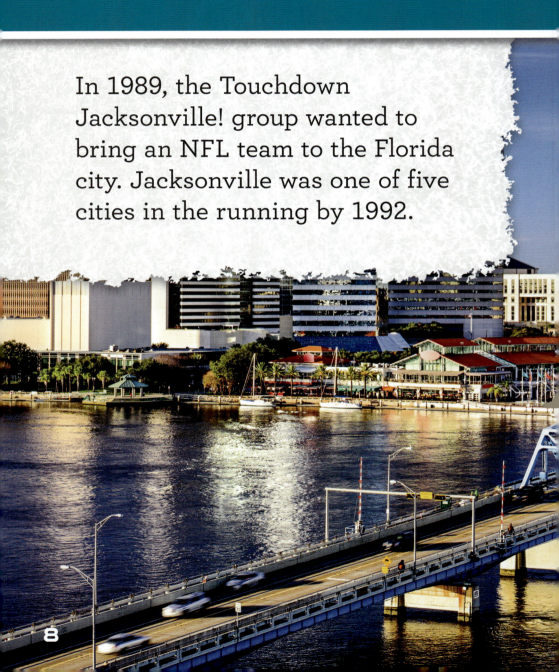

The next year, the NFL picked the Jacksonville Jaguars to join the league! Both the Jaguars and the Carolina Panthers joined the NFL in 1995 as **expansion teams**.

The Jaguars first played in September of 1995. More than 70,000 fans packed the stadium to watch the team's first home game.

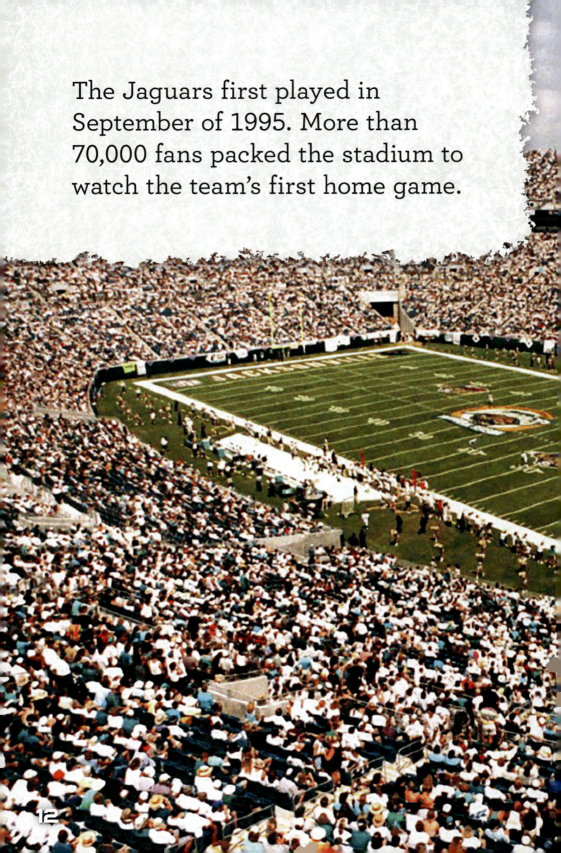

TEAM RECAPS

The Jaguars had their first winning season in 1996. They made it to the **divisional** playoff game and beat the Denver Broncos 30-27!

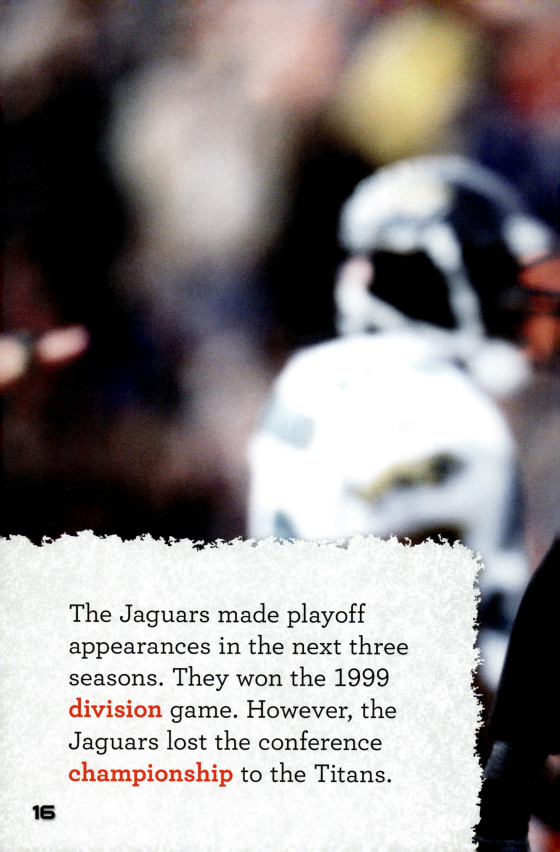

The Jaguars made playoff appearances in the next three seasons. They won the 1999 **division** game. However, the Jaguars lost the conference **championship** to the Titans.

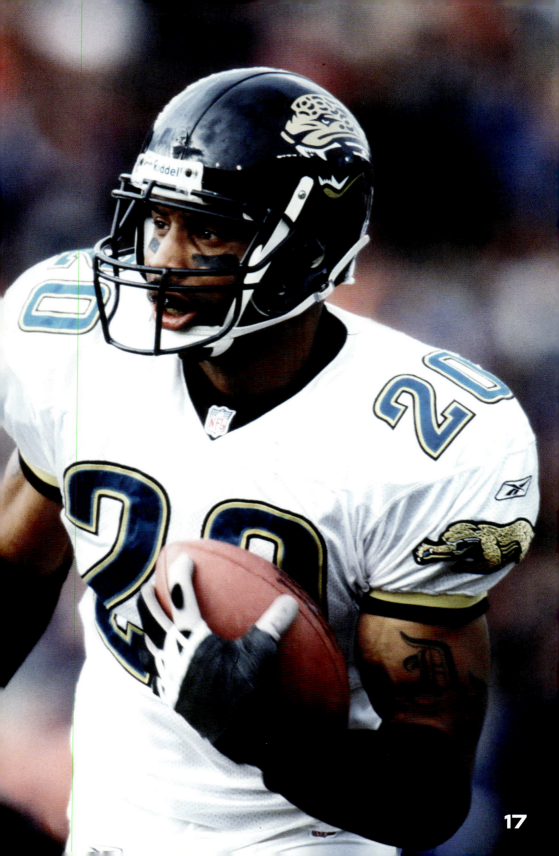

The Jaguars beat the Bills during the **Wild Card** Playoffs in 2018. They went on to Pittsburgh the next week to beat the Steelers in a huge **upset**. This earned the Jaguars a spot in the **AFC Championship** Game for the first time in 18 years!

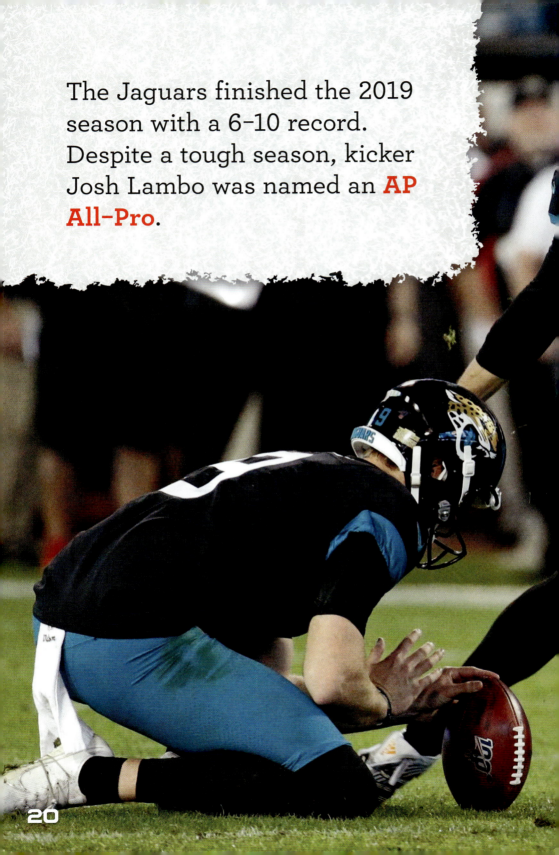

The Jaguars finished the 2019 season with a 6-10 record. Despite a tough season, kicker Josh Lambo was named an **AP All-Pro**.

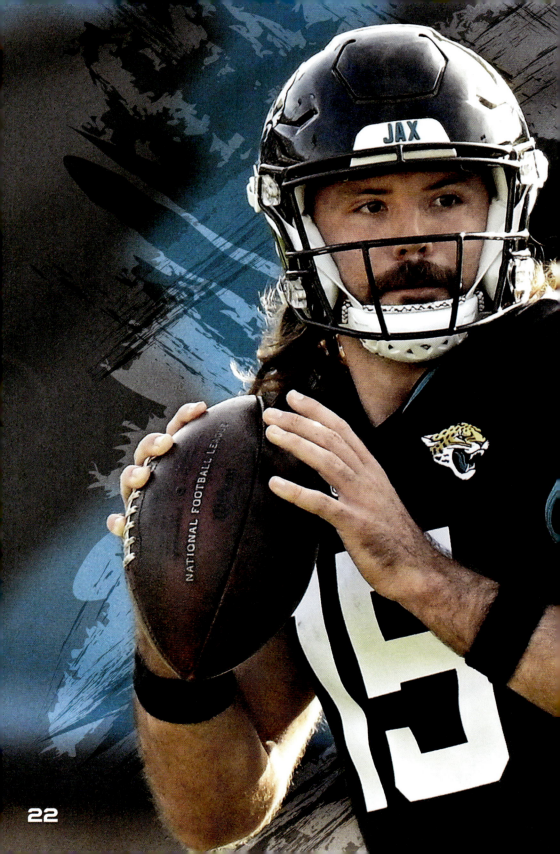

Nick Foles left the Jaguars in the 2020 season. Gardner Minshew took over starting quarterback duties. In week one, Minshew threw three touchdowns and had a 95% completion rate, an impressive feat for any QB.

The Jaguars signed Jimmy Smith in 1995. He holds the team record for most receptions, receiving yards, and touchdown catches. Many consider him to be the best receiver in the team's history!

Maurice Jones-Drew spent eight years with the Jaguars. He rushed for 1,606 yards and set a team record in 2011! He holds a team record with 81 total touchdowns as well.

Blake Bortles joined the Jaguars during the 2014 **draft**. He set many team records. Bortles once threw five touchdowns in a single game. He also had the most single season passing touchdowns and passing yards.

GLOSSARY

American Football Conference (AFC) – one of two major conferences of the NFL. Each conference contains 16 teams split into four divisions. The winner of the AFC championship plays the NFC.

AP All-Pro – an honor given by press organizations to professional NFL players that names the best player at each position during a season.

championship – a game held to find a first-place winner.

division – a group of teams who compete against each other for a championship.

draft – a process in sports to assign athletes to a certain team.

expansion team – a new football team in the NFL from a city that has not had one before.

Super Bowl – the NFL championship game, played once a year.

upset – in sports, when a team that is expected to win loses or ties a game with an underdog team.

Wild Card Round – the first round of the playoffs. Each of the two conferences send four division champions and three wild-card teams to its postseason.

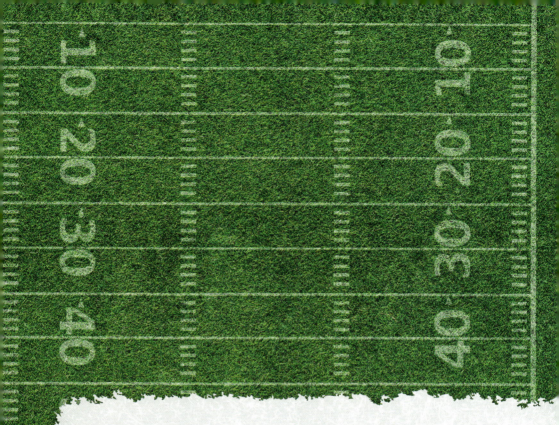

ONLINE RESOURCES

To learn more about the Jacksonville Jaguars, please visit **abdobooklinks.com** or scan this QR code. These links are routinely monitored and updated to provide the most current information available.

31

INDEX

Bills (team) 19

Bortles, Blake 29

Broncos (team) 15

championships 6, 15, 16, 19

Foles, Nick 23

Jones-Drew, Maurice 27

Lambo, Josh 20

Minshew, Gardner 23

Panthers (team) 11

Smith, Jimmy 25

Steelers (team) 19

Super Bowl 6

Titans (team) 16